"**How to do life**" fourth UK edition 2020

First published in Great Britain in 2019 by Redpump Ltd. Copyright © Chris Worth 2019.

The right of Chris Worth to be identified as the author of this work is asserted with all rights reserved.

This print perfect bound edition of "How to do life" is **ISBN 978-1-912795-25-3**

See 100days100grand.com

To Lynne, 張筱鳳

天下本無事，庸人自擾之！

"The world is simple, but some idiots make it complicated!"

—Lu Xiangxian in "The New Tang Book"

> *"I am the master of my fate;*
> *I am the captain of my soul."*
>
> —W E Henley, "Invictus"

THE MEANING OF LIFE	12
MEANING AND PURPOSE	16
BODY AND MIND ARE ONE	17
ACCEPT REALITY	19
KNOW YOUR RIGHTS	21
BANISH ENVY	24
DON'T BE A VICTIM	30
MAKE LISTS	31
READ BOOKS	32
DRINK COCKTAILS	33
TIGHTEN MEETINGS	34
DO PULLUPS	35
WALK FASTER	36
SWEAT DAILY	38
LIVE IN THE NOW	39
TRAVEL FAR	41
HAVE TO / GET TO	43
RESPECT 100-YEAR-OLD YOU	44
BE CIVILISED	45
BE HONEST	47
BE GRATEFUL	48
:-)	49

ACTION AT A DISTANCE	50
SEEK WONDER AND THRILL	51
DO STUFF	52
FIND FLOW	53
BUILD, THEN MAINTAIN	56
SET START AND END GOALS	58
BREAK PROBLEMS INTO PARTS	60
SOLVE TASKS IN SEQUENCE	61
LEVERAGE TECHNOLOGY	63
MAKE GOOD A HABIT	64
SEPARATE URGENT FROM IMPORTANT	66
MASLOW'S PYRAMID	69
BUILD YOUR BODY	72
Learn about stress	74
Eat real food	76
Focus on sleep	78
Stand up straight	79
STAYING IN SHAPE	81
Do calisthenics	85
Work out with weights	87
Train your grip	89
(Plank, hollow, and twist)	91

Think Yoga 93
(And learn to fight) 94
... DEALING WITH AGING 96
NURTURE YOUR INTELLECT 98
HOW TO LEARN 101
A-grade your three R's 104
Get into maths 106
Know your history 109
Work out physics 111
Love literature 116
HOW TO THINK 118
(Learn logic) 119
(Understand biases) 122
(Manage risk) 126
HOW TO ACT 127
DO UNTO OTHERS 130
POLITICS AND ECONOMICS 133
Understand your politics 134
Understand the economy 140
A WORD ON WEALTH 147
MAKING MONEY 149
UNDERSTANDING PEOPLE 152

UNDERSTANDING ORGANISATIONS	156
UNDERSTANDING SOCIETY	158
DISMISS THE STOOPIDS	161
DISMISS EVERYBODY	163
FAMILY AND CHILDREN	164
ON ESTEEM	168
FUCK GOVERNMENT.	169
FIND MEANINGFUL WORK	172
YOUR PURPOSE	175
ABOUT CHRIS	176

I didn't end up where I expected to in life.

Pushing 50, I'm a normal guy doing a normal job. Not a captain of industry. Not a leader of men. Not adored by millions. (Not sure I'm even in double figures there, to be honest.)

But I'm *happy*. Not in a mindless skipping-through-leaves way—it's better than that. Every day kicks off with the realisation there's stuff I want to do and I have the opportunity to do it. A sense of great fulfilment and satisfaction. What more does anyone need?

I've also "done stuff". Lived in six countries, jumped out of planes 100+ times, dived deep in diverse oceans. I've published millions of words, including my magnum opus on freelancing 100days100grand.com, and got into calisthenics and kettlebells so deeply I took instructor exams. (You don't have to be *good* at stuff to *do* stuff.) And thanks to my wife **Lynne**, I have an *amazing* family spanning the planet.

My 18-year-old self wouldn't have approved. (He was far too serious.) But I think my 6-year-old self would.

Life is *good*. And down the decades, I've learned a lot about where good comes from. So here are my notes on the basic principles of health, wealth, and happiness. Stuff that makes life the adventure it is, and our years on this pale blue dot worth the living.

I hope it brings you value.

CHRIS WORTH

THE MEANING OF LIFE

Vast volumes have been written on what life means, by exalted thinkers like Plato, Nietzsche, and Sartre.

All of whom you can safely ignore.

(Well, you can read *Sophie's World* if you like. That's a decent summary.)

Why? Because the giants of philosophy got it wrong. Life is *not* some anguished struggle. And pipe-smoking miserablists using tricks of language to demonstrate their cleverness *aren't* the right people to tell you how to live it.

The meaning of life is found in an idea that unites all living things. In fact, the *only* idea that includes everything that lives, while excluding everything *not* alive. Here it is:

==Living things *move towards value*.==

A flower turns to the sun. A tiger chases prey. A bacterium orients itself towards the sugar molecule.

No non-living thing chases what it wants. No non-living thing "wants" anything at all. But every single *living* thing takes action to *pursue what it values*.

In this behaviour is the meaning of life.

(Note: "value" is what matters to the *individual*, not its society or species. You cannot breathe, eat, or sleep for another; these are things you must do for *yourself* to gain value. The act of living is an individual enterprise, not a collective one.)

Of course, breathing, eating, and sleeping are basic. But the principle applies to *any* life goal. Satisfaction is not found in what others do for you, but in what *you* do for *yourself*. Of your own volition and with your own abilities, in accordance with your nature.

Denying this principle denies life. A tree sheltered from the wind it evolved to withstand will wither, no matter how rich its soil. A caged zoo animal unable to prowl and hunt will pace endlessly as it loses its mind. Rich kids spending Daddy's cash end up in rehab.

In other words, when you're *prevented* from pursuing what you value—by laws or leg irons—you start to die. From frustration, helplessness, or plain boredom.

Many people you know are effectively dead already; they just haven't stopped moving yet.

Think of the happiest people you know: they're the

ones doing what matters most to *them*, for their *own* satisfaction.

So that's the meaning of life: ==pursue what you value==. Choose goals that matter to *you*, and strive for them with your *own* talents. Don't ask for handouts, or coerce others into providing for you; that's not the nature of life.

The successful *state* of living—**happiness**—flows wholly from this simple principle.

That's Lesson 1 of doing life. And if you don't read further, it's all you need.

MEANING AND PURPOSE

Next, look up into the night sky. You can see a few thousand stars. But our galaxy contains 100bn of 'em. And the universe has as many galaxies. There may even be a multiplicity of universes, a "multiverse" infinite in all directions.

And none of it cares about you.

You are nothing. The universe has no plan for you. But that's not a downer. It's *great*. Because when you understand the universe has no meaning or purpose deeper than existing, it lets you live your life on terms true to yourself. To create your *own* meaning.

To do life successfully, realise that finding a purpose in it is up to *you*. ==You decide what meaning means.==

BODY AND MIND ARE ONE

Of course, you need something to do life *with*. That something is your mind and body.

"Something" is singular, because contrary to much of Western philosophy (less so Eastern) mind and body are **one and the same**.

That kilo-plus of grey matter inside your head *guides* your body, but it's also *part* of it. Your brain sluices out chemicals and electrical impulses to make your body do things, but is also *affected* by those same sloshes and sparks, in endless feedback loops. Thoughts create feelings and feelings create thoughts. (Think of feelings as the thoughts of the body, and thoughts as the feelings of the mind.) Your mental state is a physical state; there is no "you" separate from your body.

And the greatest mystery of philosophy—**consciousness**—is simply an emergent effect of those billions of networked neurons, defined by and contained within them.

This sparking, sloshing, shaking squishbag is your tool for doing life. So it's worth developing the best mind and body you can. In the understanding that each benefits the other, yin and yang.

This means devoting effort to your **health** and **intellect**, and using them to do productive **work** that gives you a sense of **purpose**.

These subjects take up most of this little book.

ACCEPT REALITY

There's another attribute of this mind-and-body of yours. It's *real*.

You are made of atoms, joined into molecules, all mingling and jiggling in accordance with the laws of physics. So is everything else. Atoms and molecules, gravity and electromagnetism, the strong and weak nuclear forces **exist**; they are *not* theoretical constructs, *not* "all in our minds". Everything real is subject to them. Anything *not* subject to the laws of physics is irrelevant, because it doesn't exist.

You are not supernatural, and nor is anything else. And no hoping or praying will change that. (Sorry, gods and ghosts.)

So to take effective action in the real world, first ==accept reality==. It's all there is. A is A.

"Nature, to be commanded, must first be obeyed"— Francis Bacon

Sounds limiting? It's not. It is *empowering*.

Because when you understand nature is subject to laws—many of which are known—you gain the opportunity to understand it, make use of it, turn it to your advantage as you pursue what you value.

You exist. The supernatural does not. Everything that exists is subject to natural laws. Change is made by action, not wishful thinking.

Accept reality.

KNOW YOUR RIGHTS

Your life belongs to you, and your life is contained within your body. So you also own your body. In other words, you're an *individual with rights*. Which is great.

But while great, a surprising number of political economies don't accept it. They believe they own you, that your life somehow belongs to "The State". (See "Fuck Government" later on.) And if you believe them, they've got you over a barrel.

So to do life, it's important to *understand* your rights. Not those conferred by laws, but those derived from first principles, *independent* of gods and governments. *They're* the ones worth fighting for.

This involves knowing what rights *are* and *aren't*.

First up, understand all rights derive from a fundamental one: the ==right to life==. Others don't have the right to kill you. (That includes the State: although some places still have the death penalty, it's an instrument of power, not punishment.)

All genuine rights—ownership of your mind and body, the freedom to move towards value—derive from this one axiom.

Second, rights belong to the *individual*, not the collective. Once you start granting rights to groups over individuals—giving one collective an advantage over another—you're setting the scene for conflict.

(The failure to respect this principle explains most laws, wars, and suffering down the centuries.)

Third: nobody has the right to force you to do

something for them against your will, because that's an infringement of *your* rights. ==You are an end in yourself, not a means to the ends of others==.

(This means education and healthcare, while nice-to-haves, are not "rights". They're goals.)

Protecting your rights as an individual is the *only* moral purpose of government. (Pity they all get too big for their boots.)

So as Lesson 2 of doing life, understand what rights are . . . and aren't. And the next time someone starts bleating about theirs, check they know too.

BANISH ENVY

Remember the Seven Deadly Sins? Lust, gluttony, greed, sloth, wrath, envy, pride?

There's only one you need to get rid of: **envy**.

(Greed is good: it's a reason to pursue your goals. So is pride: satisfaction in what you've achieved. And a bit of lust can be *awesome*. Phwoar!)

But the green-eyed monster? That's the one that stops you accepting reality, understanding rights, all the beliefs that free you to pursue what you value.

Most envy, of course, is about wealth. So to banish it from your life, *understand how wealth works*.

Understanding wealth involves two bits of maths: **Power Laws** and **Normal Distributions**.

Power Laws in brief: what's big gets bigger faster. Normal Distributions in brief: everything clusters around the average.

(The 80:20 Rule, also known as "Pareto's Principle", is a Power Law: a graph getting ever steeper at the right. The bell-shaped curve describing spreads within a population is a Normal Distribution.)

A huge number of natural phenomena are governed by these two mathematical concepts, from weather patterns to animal populations.

The pointy bit: in society, ==wealth follows a Power Law, but human ability is a Normal Distribution==.

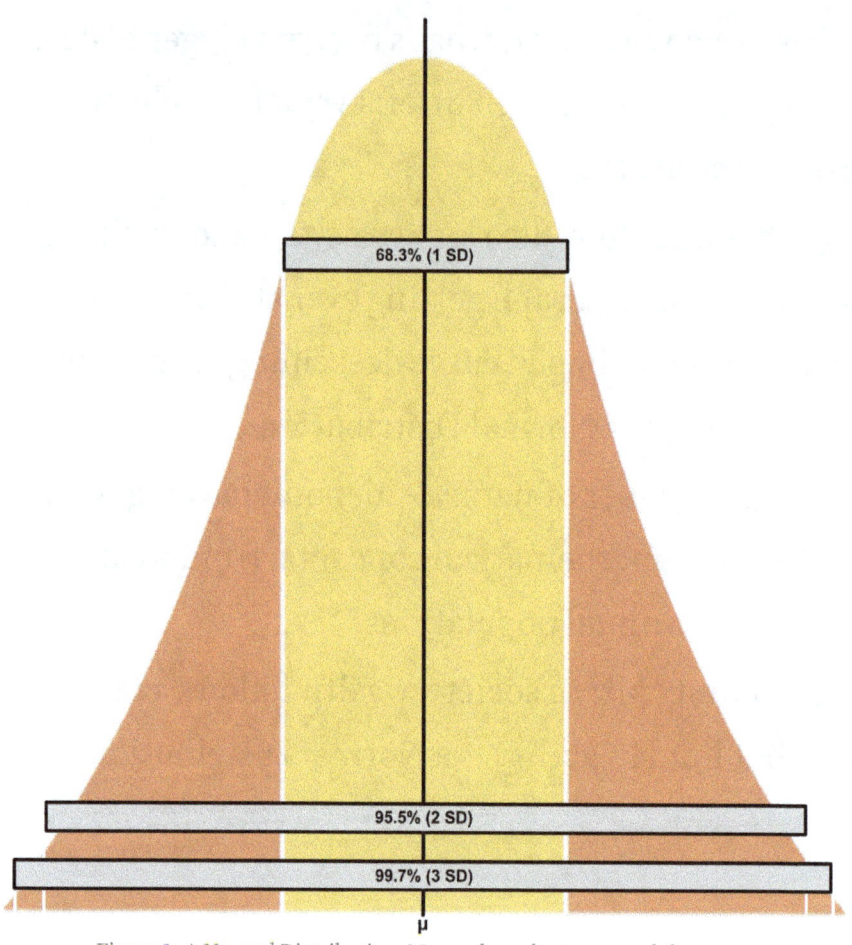

Figure 1: A Normal Distribution. Most values cluster around the mean.

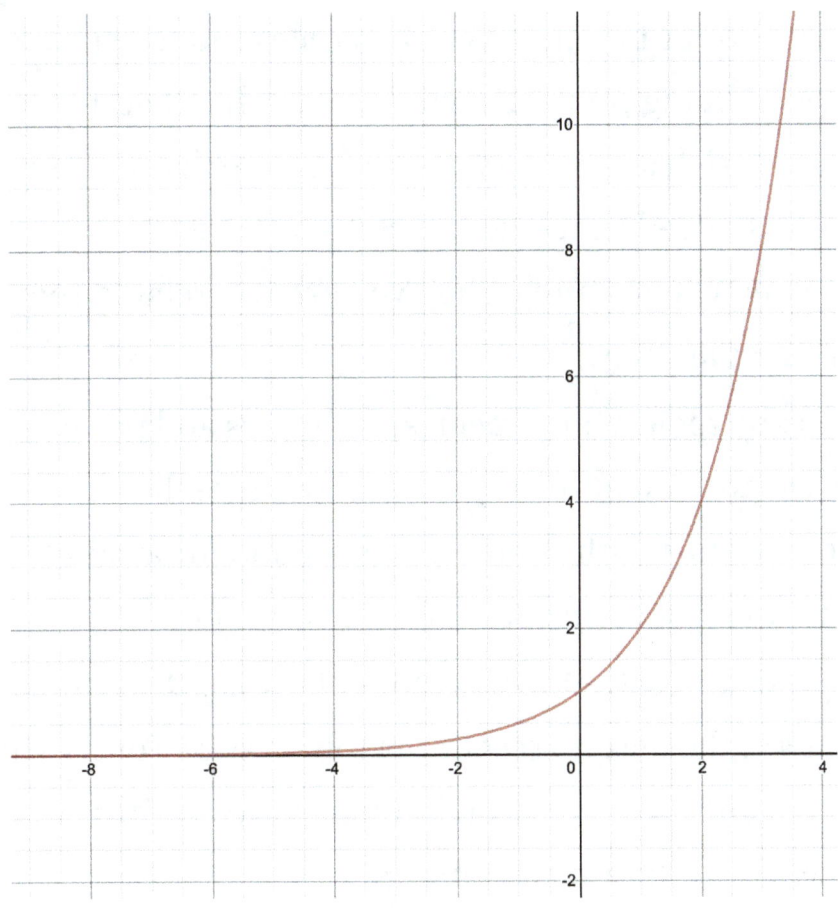

Figure 2: Power Laws. Whoever gets most, gets more.

The Power Law means rich people tend to get richer, *without* being proportionately more able. The guy twice as rich as you *might* be twice as smart. But the guy a hundred times richer *isn't* a hundred times smarter. (Smart and rich have never correlated that strongly, anyway.)

In any society, any species, resources and power accrue to a few at the top. Mostly because they had more to start with. Which might sound unfair. But don't worry, because it's the same for them.

Percentiles 81-96 are jealous of the top 4%. Among that 4%, the lower 3 resent the top 1. And so on, within the 1%, until you get to eight men at the top owning as much as the bottom six billion.

And even up there in the stratosphere of wealth, No.

2 is still jealous of No. 1. It's envy all the way up.

So what if, understanding this, you decided to accept reality (because you can't change it) ... and just ==let go of all envy==, making a decision to not judge your own success by anybody else's? (The rich have their own problems, anyway.)

You can't do anything about the laws of nature. Use this understanding to overcome envy, and you've passed Level 99 in life's game.

So the last of our "first four"—life, rights, reality, envy—is to never give space in your heart to the green-eyed monster.

Overcoming envy is how you make health, wealth, and happiness happen for *yourself*.

DON'T BE A VICTIM

Everything that happens to you is your fault.

Even if it isn't.

Accepting responsibility for the way things turn out lets you own your life, as you own your mind and body. When you realise that the only person who can change your life is *you*, it fosters an innate self-confidence and hones your ability to *take action*.

So as a general rule, live by your own hand. Blame nobody for what happens. Pursue what you value, and exchange value for value when you transact with others. Don't be a victim. Even if you are one.

In fact, this is when it works best.

MAKE LISTS

When doing stuff, there are some side skills that let you do more of it in less time. The simplest of them—one *everyone* needs—is making lists.

If you don't make them: start now. If you think you don't need to: think again.

The simple act of writing things down conveys both the size of your tasks and the best order to do them in. Ticking off items on a list also gives you a positive little tingle, the feeling you're moving forward in life.

Make lists.

READ BOOKS

More on learning later, but for now Lesson 3 of doing life: **get good at learning from books**.

Books. Not YouTube videos. Not social media. Not podcasts. (Although all these have their place.)

A proper book, written by an expert with chapters and an index, is the essence of learning. The ability to understand a text, integrate its concepts, and apply them generally is the mark of an educated person.

Getting good at reading and getting good at reading *books* are different skills. But the latter hones a hugely useful skill for doing life: **the ability to learn**.

So read one book a week, minimum. One *good* book.

DRINK COCKTAILS

Sounds odd, in all this high-falutin' life-doin' stuff? Not really.

Cocktails are doing life in a nutshell. They're creative. Interesting. *Fun*.

And in contrast to our plug-'n-play, shrink-wrapped, easy-cook world, they take a bit of effort. You've got to gather your bottles. Check you've got ice. And fruit. And a shaker.

Develop a taste for cocktails, and you're developing a taste for life's deeper, more complex mysteries. And enjoying greater rewards as a result.

TIGHTEN MEETINGS

At work, no skill is more useful than knowing how to do meetings successfully.

"Success" is *not* how many people come. Nor how much they talk. And *certainly* not how long it lasts.

A meeting has one of two goals: to execute a task, or to make a decision. Invite the minimum number to get either done: no interlopers, no special guests, nobody curious. Stay on agenda, set precise start and finish times, and lock out latecomers. They'll soon learn.

A focus on meeting discipline, like drinking cocktails, has great carry-over into the rest of life. Although it's rarely wise to do both at the same time.

DO PULLUPS

More on fitness later, but for now: the most useful test of whether you're living up to the potential of the human animal is to **do pullups**.

The ability to lift your bodyweight against gravity is empowering. It wakes the big muscles on your back most white-collar workers rarely use. Accordingly, ==do pullups every day==. Even if it's only a set of three. Or two. Or *one*.

Build up gradually to daily pullups, using the progressive calisthenics methods you'll see later—the core text is Paul Wade's "Convict Conditioning"—and you're setting yourself up for a healthy life.

WALK FASTER

Are you one of those people who think everyone walks too slow, and you're constantly swerving and jostling along pavements to get past?

Carry on doing it.

Your walking speed is a proxy for health. Because it uses all the bits of your body that atrophy in over-comfortable modern lifestyles: your glutes and spine, lung function and eyesight, reaction speed.

A walking speed of two metres a second is "fast". 1.2m/s or less is "slow". People whose walking speed is closer to slow than fast look older, die younger, have smaller brains. (Yes, really.). Slowpokes also suffer a higher risk of dementia and decline.

Walking, as a basic human skill, uses all the parts of your body in the right way. It improves balance, breathing, burns more calories, improves muscle tone. And because you'll get where you're going faster, you'll have more time to get more stuff done.

So measure your walking speed, and if it's slow, work to improve it. Particularly if you're 45 or over. (That's the age where it gets *really* important.)

Walk faster.

SWEAT DAILY

Love your sweat.

"Detoxing" is a myth. But good, healthy sweating still makes you feel *great*. It clears your pores, refreshes your body, keeps your skin clean. Sweating is an evolved body function; not doing it for weeks on end is unnatural.

So when you're taking care of your other organs with the core, cardio, and grip work you'll learn later, the biggest organ of all (your skin) will take care of itself.

Every day, do something that makes you sweat. It even fosters gratitude—in this case, for hot water and an invigorating scrub.

LIVE IN THE NOW

"Yesterday is history. Tomorrow is mystery. But today is a gift. That's why we call it the present."—Bil Keane

Life is distraction. The ping of an email. Buzz of a phone. Hubbub of the office cube farm. Which is why so many of us spend our days clenched, flinching, and twitching with tension and tics over what comes next. Buddhists call it the "monkey mind", swinging from thought to thought without really *thinking*.

Everyone ponders the past, worries about the future. But the future isn't here yet. And the past is done. Why replay bad memories? Why worry about what you can't control? Life unfolds in the *present*.

So while forward planning is a worthy goal, and your memories are what make you unique, never forget you *live* in the here and now. Don't let time rush past unobserved or unexperienced.

Every day, spend a few minutes doing nothing but feeling yourself breathe, listening to your own heartbeat. Noticing everything, but judging nothing. Call it meditation, mindfulness, whatever: it works. There's calm in being fascinated with whatever's in front of you, right now.

Living in the now helps you control over your thoughts. And since mind and body are one, that means greater control over your body too.

TRAVEL FAR

To gain knowledge of the world, you need to get out in that world. To do this, try and travel every year. Ideally, to a place you don't know, somewhere that scares you a little.

There's a lot of it. The grandeur of old Europe. The seething cities of Asia. The mottled bones of Chile's Atacama; the energy of Brazil's *favelas*. The rainbow colours of the Mediterranean coast; the searingly beautiful landscapes of Europe's Alps, Canada's Rockies, Asia's Himalayas. The lonely roads of America's southwest; the dead red centre of Australia; the island patchworks of Greece and Indonesia. The intoxicating flavours of Thailand and Vietnam. The dialect-defined regions of China, distinct as the nations of Europe. They are all incredible; every travel experience will expand your mind.

And that's without even going to extremes. Learn to ski, so you can get up mountains. Learn to dive, so you can explore oceans. See how life conquers all, from parched deserts to soaked coasts; visit the citadels lost in the sands of Egypt and the societies forgotten in the forests of Mexico. And understand that whatever nature gives away, it will one day take back.

Of course, you'll never see them all, and that's the point. The upside is you'll never run out of them. Travel is a lifelong adventure where the real objective is the journey.

To do life: Live deep. Travel far. Engage creatively.

HAVE TO / GET TO

As you pursue your goals, you'll be faced with stuff you don't want to do. There's no way around this. There is, however, a simple trick to make it easier.

Instead of groaning, "I *have* to do this . . ."

Punch the air and exclaim, "I *get* to do this!"

The application letter that boosts your chance of a great job? You *get* to write it. The paintwork that'll make your house like new? You *get* to do that. The breakup conversation that saves you a lifetime of pain? That's up to *you*. Think first of the positive outcome, not the pain of getting started.

Swapping out "have to" for "get to" puts the bad thing in context with the good thing it enables. Use it.

RESPECT 100-YEAR-OLD YOU

Life is full of big decisions. Because everything carries a cost. Sometimes we don't do things we know we really want to do, because the cost seems too high.

Here's how to solve such self-limiting beliefs.

Imagine yourself aged 100, looking back on your life. That thing you didn't do . . . at 100, will you regret *not* doing it?

If so, you should do it. Whether it's something big, like starting a business, or something even bigger, like starting a family.

Your 100-year-old self is wiser than you. So listen.

BE CIVILISED

Humans have two systems for making decisions: System 1 and System 2. (A theory formalised by Daniel Kahnemann in "Thinking, Fast and Slow".)

S1 is our instincts and emotions, coded in our ancient brains. It's the flight-or-flight response. The involuntary reaction. The conclusion jumped to.

S2 is more calculating. It's slower, thoughtful, using logic and abstract reasoning to understand different outcomes. It's how you do maths, engage in debate, focus your attention on problems.

Someone habitually using their S2, rather than letting their S1 guide their life, is a **civilised person**. Who can imagine the world from the perspective of another, and integrate different view*points* into a coherent world*view*. Who's open to different opinions, conflicting cultures, our wonderful diversity.

Being civilised doesn't need formal education, or wealth, or "breeding". It's a skill, and can be learned. So in a world where that rustle in the bushes probably *isn't* something that sees you as lunch, learn to ==stop and think== before you act.

Civilised people can be reasoned with. Which is why Lesson 4 of doing life is to strive for civility. It's the rule for managing yourself and dealing successfully with others by finding the win-win.

Be civilised.

BE HONEST

It really *is* the best policy.

Speak truth. To power. To others. To yourself.

Honesty is a get-out-of-jail free card. At work, it can excuse errors. At home, it can solve relationship issues. And inside your head, it cuts conflict.

Being honest does not mean being brutal. Even the hardest truths can be communicated with tact. (That's why improving your *writing* is a great skill for doing life. More on that and other skills later.)

And that includes *white* lies. Just because your heart's in the right place doesn't mean your head is.

BE GRATEFUL

Life isn't serious. So you shouldn't *take* anything too seriously. Least of all yourself. Instead, be *grateful*.

If you've got a roof over your head, enough to eat, and your health, you're already a winner. Everything else is a bonus.

And it doesn't take much to climb the ladder. A net worth of less than five thousand US dollars puts you in the wealthiest half of humanity. You only need $100,000 to get into the *top ten percent*.

Think of what you've got. Vaccines. Cheap flights. The Internet. Now is the best time to be alive. Ever.

So be thankful for what you've got, and don't take life too seriously. Make gratitude your attitude.

:-)

Since mind and body are one, and what you do with your body affects your mind, it's worthwhile doing a simple physical action many times a day: **smile**.

When good things happen, you smile. But the opposite's true too: when you smile, good things happen. The connection between what you do and how you feel works both ways.

Smiling anchors a good experience: you did it the last time you felt happy. Smiling without any other reason will bring the good times back.

To maintain a cheerful and sunny disposition, ☺.

ACTION AT A DISTANCE

One metric of success is how capably you can act at a distance. The further away your actions are felt, the greater the dent you'll make in the universe.

Any fool can swing his fist. But fewer can use a crossbow. And fewer still can command an army. Countless cooks can work a grill, but few can franchise a steakhouse chain. Many can write code; few can create a platform that enables new technologies.

Next time you feel frustrated, ponder if it's because the impact of your actions isn't what you want it to be. Could a change of tactics increase your radius of effectiveness? Distance is the metric.

SEEK WONDER AND THRILL

Doing life successfully means staying interested.

Wonder and thrill are the lats and glutes of the emotional spectrum. (More on these muscles later.) They're essential for a positive sense of self, yet functionally absent in many. The lack of them is why you see 25-year olds commuting with grey faces and furrowed brows. But they're also why you see 90-year olds enjoying life with the joys of a child.

When did you last feel awestruck? If it's more than a week, work on recapturing that sense of life's marvels you once had. It's in there somewhere.

DO STUFF

Let's bring things together. To move towards value, you've got to *do stuff*.

Doing stuff that intrigues you—no matter what that stuff is—is how you broaden your horizons and discover what you're good at, what you like, where your deepest passions and purpose lie.

Reading books is what you do with your head; doing stuff is the work of your hands. But it's a big world out there. With a lot to explore. So how do you know if the stuff you're doing is the *right* stuff or not?

Easy. The goal of doing stuff is to find something—anything—that gets you into a **flow state**.

FIND FLOW

Remember the last time you felt on top of the world while performing a task? When you felt challenged but energised, finding the process as meaningful as the outcome? When time seemed not to matter, with whole hours going by in a heartbeat?

That's **flow**, defined by Mihaly Csikszentmihalyi. Joy in the doing. It's a balance of skill and challenge, with the feeling you're adding to yourself as you do it.

Flow is the source of all rewarding activity, all obsessive hobbies, all your best work. Everything you find really, really interesting.

Finding it has four parts.

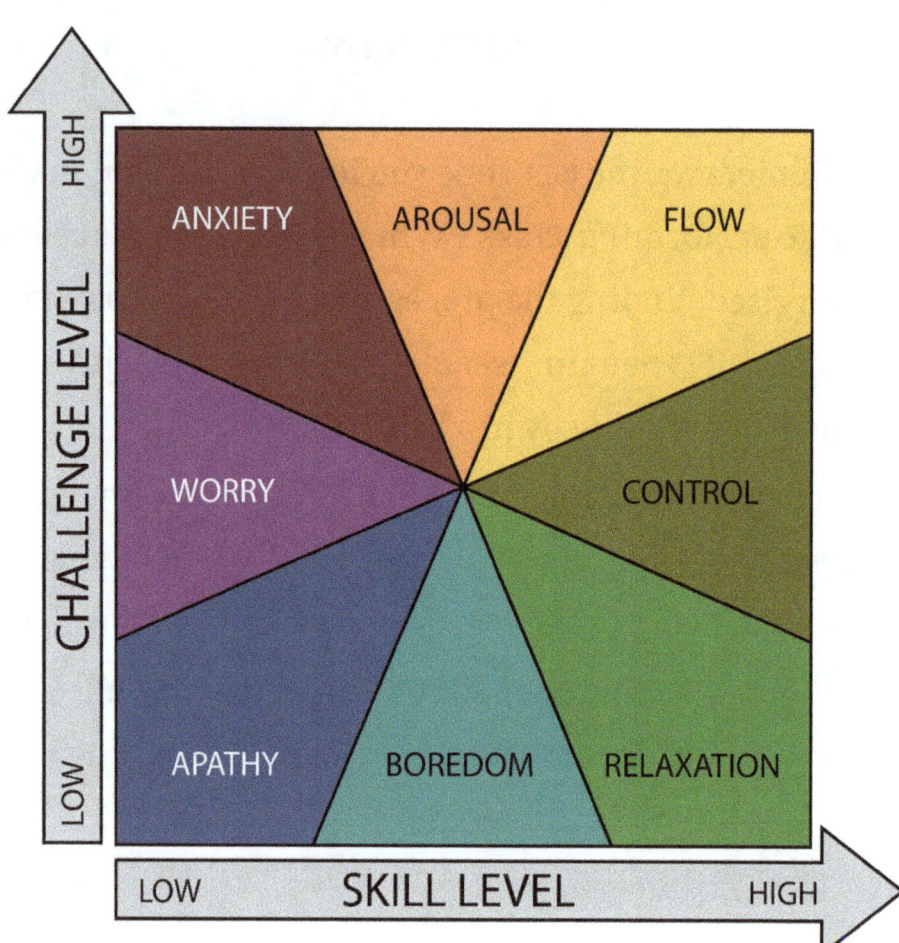

First, you'll need a **stretch goal**. Small or large, but beyond your current abilities. An outcome you'll have to work a bit harder for.

Second, **existing expertise**. The skills to approach that task, whatever its level of difficulty. If you've just learned to hold a spade, your stretch goal is a hole.

Third, **clear feedback**. Something—maybe a person, maybe the task itself—that returns information on how you're doing. Providing your milestones.

Fourth and last, **personal growth**. That feeling of great satisfaction on completion.

==Flow is the state of mind that leads to happiness.== Lesson whatever-it-was: **do stuff** and **find your flow**.

BUILD, THEN MAINTAIN

Everything you do has a **build phase**—when you're planning or creating—and a **maintenance phase**, when you're living with the results.

(At work, it's the difference between being on a project and "Business as Usual", or BAU.)

The pointy bit: **building** takes time and energy, because you're committing a creative act, bringing something new into the world. **Maintenance** takes a lot less effort, since you're just keeping what's already there topped up.

So as you sweat your way to your goals, remember that **the build phase will be worth it**. Once you've reached your successful state, it might take only minutes in the gym to keep the body that cost two years to build. When you've learned calculus, it'll seem breezily easy, and you'll forget how weird a concept "instantaneous change" is.

The build phase is an investment. And investments take time to bear fruit. During the build phase it might feel like you're getting nowhere. Which is why so many give up. But maintaining? That's enjoying the compound interest.

The difference between building and maintaining is why many successful people seem to be living successful lives effortlessly. It's true they may not be making much effort *now*. But they did to get there.

SET START AND END GOALS

Any task is best approached with its end in mind. But when it comes to defining what that end is, many times, you'll find you can't answer. Which means you should stop until you can.

So whenever you start a task, think: ==what does success look like?==

This means treating every task as a *project*.

"Start where you are. Use what you have. Do what you can." – Arthur Ashe, athlete

Call "where you are" **Situation A**. Call your goal **Situation B**. Defining your endpoints kicks off your plan to get from one to the other. How many actions need completing and in what sequence, what milestones demonstrate progress, the timeline you'll do it on and the resources you need to get there.

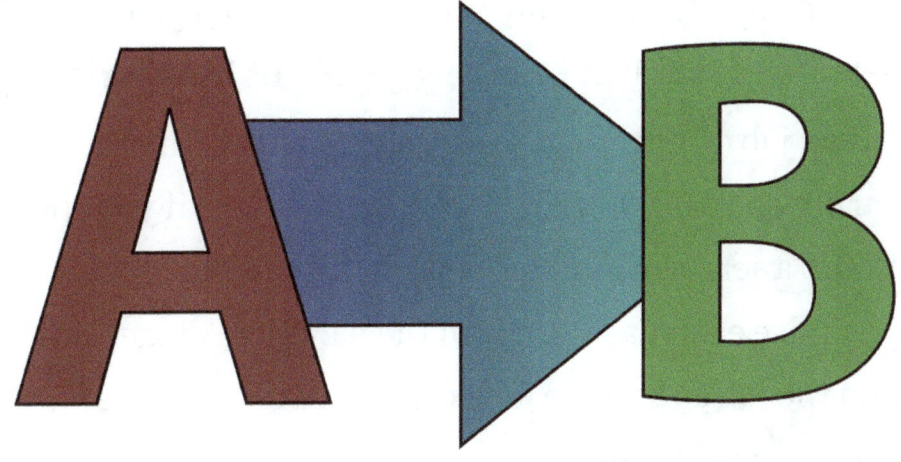

If you can make a list and set priorities, you can write a project plan. And it starts with writing down where you are, and where you want to be.

BREAK PROBLEMS INTO PARTS

Of course, going from A to B may be a *big* project. So get into the habit of **breaking problems into parts**.

Any job of work—changing your life, getting fit, earning a £100,000 income—is achievable if you split it into a series of smaller tasks in logical sequence. As you solve each part, you join the parts back together, and the job as a whole looks easier. And then—hey presto—you've done it.

Drill down. Chunk up. In other words, ==differentiate then integrate==. Like learning and thinking—and, indeed, consciousness itself—that's all doing life is.

SOLVE TASKS IN SEQUENCE

You can't build the life of your dreams all at once. In fact, thinking big is about *not* making a huge change today. It's about *little* changes, *sustained over time*.

Are you ready for that paradigm-busting, earth-shaking, life-altering decision today? Probably not. But you can avoid that second cookie with lunch.

So once you've broken a problem into parts, solve each part **in sequence**. *Not* all at once. Treat each as an individual task, complete in itself. Then "level up", with a sense of completion.

If you improve 2% a month, you'll be twice as good in three years. A great result, for not much outlay.

But it works both ways. If you let yourself go and

decline 2% a month, you'll be barely half as good in the same time.

Which for many will be the harder kick-in-the-pants. Because while incremental success through regular action is mindful and measurable, incremental decline is barely noticeable until it matters.

So plan each goal as a series of steps in logical sequence. Then take the first.

LEVERAGE TECHNOLOGY

Technology isn't taking our jobs and making society poorer as too many believe. It's making us *rich beyond our wildest dreams*.

Rockefeller, Vanderbilt, and JP Morgan never had pocket supercomputers connecting them to billions. Applications that empower productivity. A thousand textbooks on a thin grey slate. Or worldwide delivery networks, or thousands of airports to use, or . . .

. . . you get the idea. There's an *unbelievable* amount of stuff out there that extends your abilities far beyond arm's length, creating countless opportunities to reach your goals. Technology is not a threat: it's the truest declaration of human potential. Embrace it.

MAKE GOOD A HABIT

You know when you've done something good. Learned something, read a book, managed a gym visit. But it's harder to turn that good into a *habit*.

Good habits—consistent best practice—are the difference between a humdrum life and one lived effectively. But when it comes to forming *good* habits, it's helpful to start with your *bad* ones.

Author James Clear believes bad habits stem from stress and boredom (two flow-stoppers) and that the way to get rid of a bad habit is to ==replace it with a good one==, not try to delete it. Because bad habits have the same effects as good ones: they provide a *benefit*. Cigarettes relieve stress; sweets give you energy.

So the key to forming *good* habits is to look at the benefit each *bad* habit already provides, and find a *good* habit that gives you something similar.

Instead of a smoking break, do two minutes of breathing exercises. Instead of candy, keep carrots and hummus in the fridge. Instead of picking your fingernails, do ten reps with a grip trainer.

It'll feel hard at first. But all it takes is a little nudge whenever you get the urge. And then you get *used* to it.

How long does it take to turn a bad habit into a good one? About three months. That's a long time—but not *that* long. Call it 100 days of nudges.

Take those 100 days to form good habits, and they'll pay you back your whole life.

SEPARATE URGENT FROM IMPORTANT

Most people's lives are submerged in busywork. 200 emails a day, endless hours in meetings; the drive to do *something* overriding what *matters*.

So another side skill for doing life successfully is to differentiate between what your S2 wants you to do, and what tugs at your S1 to be done now.

In other words, seeing past what's *urgent* and deciding what's genuinely *important*.

A useful tactic for life is to divide your To-Do list into four parts on the **Eisenhower Matrix**, named for the President who used them.

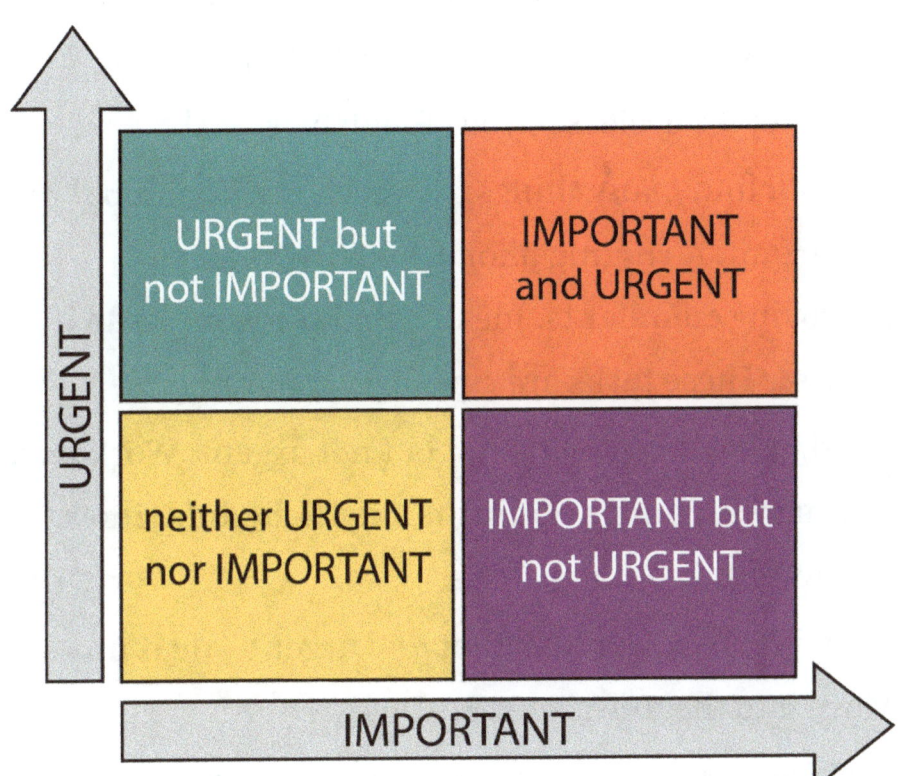

If your action item is neither important *nor* urgent, your response is simple: **don't do it**. Delete it from your life; it's useless to you. Tough luck, task.

You'll find many things, however, are urgent but not important. A ringing phone, booking flights, approving comments. Ideally, find someone to **do it for you**. These tasks are ripe for outsourcing.

Others may be important but not urgent. Workouts, dealing with bills, phoning family. **Schedule times** to do these and get them done.

And if it's both important *and* urgent—**do it now**. Move it to the top of your To-Do list.

"What is urgent is seldom important, and what is important is seldom urgent."

MASLOW'S PYRAMID

Let's recap. The meaning of life is the pursuit of value. And your mind and body, an individual with rights, is your means of achieving the successful state of life: happiness. (*If* you drink cocktails, run tight meetings, take baby steps, and so on.)

What stops you from getting there, RIGHT NOW?

Reality.

Pursuing your goals is a *journey*, not a one-off action. There are milestones between you and what you value most.

You can't build a house if you don't have enough to eat. Or run your business if you're running off raiders each day. Doing life means doing things *in order*.

Your first moves toward value are about the basics: food, water, somewhere to sleep. (This is as far as most creatures on Earth get, so count yourself lucky already.) *Then* you can start looking ahead: building skills, amassing resources, investing for the future. After that, work on the relationships that provide opportunities to create and exchange value. And so on.

So doing life means levelling up, making progress, building achievement on achievement.

The ultimate goal is **self-actualisation**, where you're empowered to pursue your true passions and purpose. It's the pointy bit of Abraham Maslow's **Hierarchy of Needs.** The rest of this book riffs on the layers.

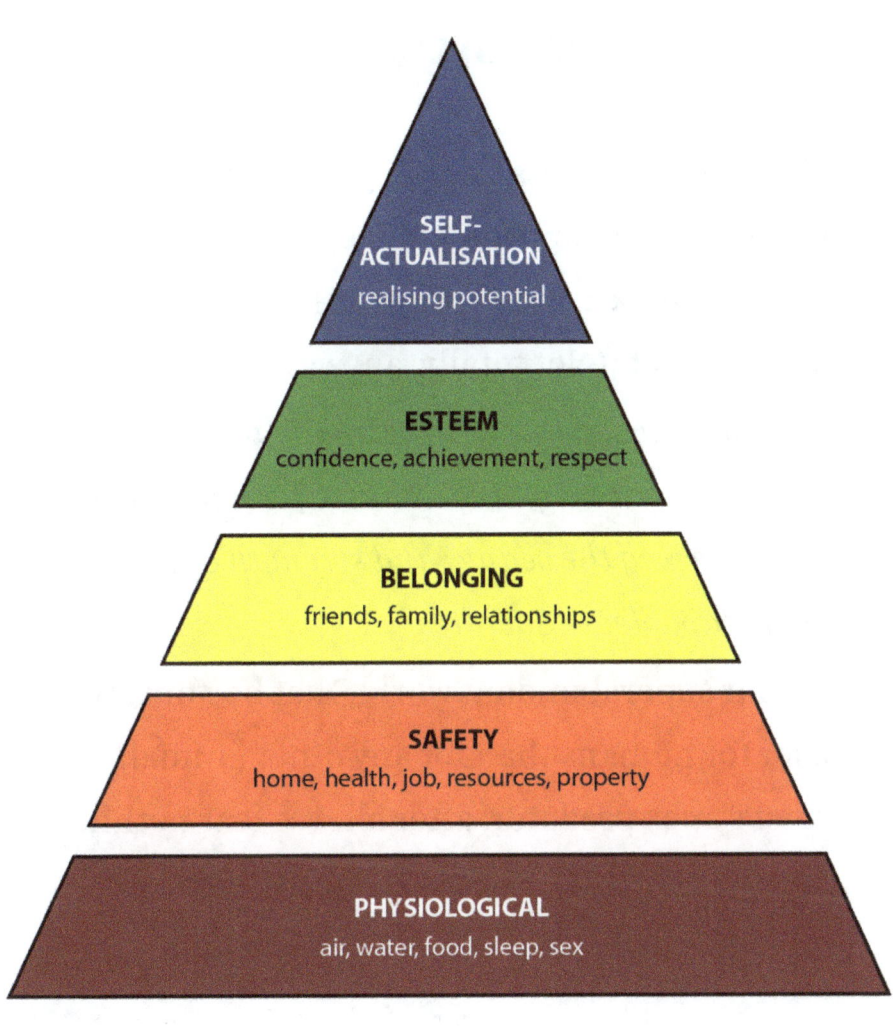

BUILD YOUR BODY

You make progress on your journey towards your goals by using your **mind**. Since your mind is part of your body, making that body the best it can be is *not* a vanity project. (Not totally, anyway.)

"No man has the right to be an amateur in the matter of physical training. It is a shame for a man to grow old without seeing the beauty and strength of which his body is capable." – Socrates

In our superabundant world, that bottom layer is easier for humans than for any other animal. We're the planet's apex predator, after all. We fear nothing. (Except each other.) But that doesn't mean the problems go away. Rather, it *changes* them.

But before this book gets into the fitness stuff, let's look at the stuff that *prevents* you building your best body. The developed-world human does too many of the wrong things: eats too much, sleeps too little, and sits around a lot. And above all worries too much, leading to that constant, low-level **stress** that builds over time into a killer of happiness, productivity, and life itself.

Here's how to change that.

Learn about stress

Two factors feature big in stressed individuals: **inflammation** and **oxidisation**.

Inflammation is an immune response. We can't do without it: soreness and redness are part of healing from injury. But it *is* a strain on the body, which is why recovery takes time. And when it goes on forever—instead of stopping after a few days—you get *chronic inflammation*. Constant, low-level stress that eats away at your health over time.

Riding tandem is **oxidisation**. (Yes, we rust.) Of course, the body needs oxygen—but a surfeit of *free radicals*, oxygen atoms with dangling bonds looking for trouble, wreaks havoc on the body. Too many free radicals are the other side of stress: fatigue, premature aging, proneness to ill health.

==Modern lifestyles—bullshit jobs, processed food, unhealthy air, screens instead of sleep—are full of stressors that cause both.==

Not everyone is driven to attain peak fitness. But most want to feel healthy. So to kickstart your journey to better health, read up on inflammation and oxidisation, the twin killers eating away at your energy and vitality. Make banishing *them* your motivation for establishing health.

That's the "why". Now let's look at the "how".

Eat real food

For many of us, the problem with food isn't scarcity but abundance. So at the base of Maslow's Pyramid, when you're honing the body and mind to level up, focus on getting *good* food, not *enough* food.

First, understand what food is. There are **foods**, which are recognisably from field or stream, and there are **products**, which are from factories. Prefer the former. There are no "superfoods".

Michael Pollan's mantra works: *Eat food. Mostly plants. Not too much.*

Here's the rule: you can eat anything you like, in any volume, as often as you want . . . *if you make it yourself from raw.*

That means no pre-packaged calories like cakes. No processed meats like burgers. And nothing with a list of ingredients that look like codewords. Bake it, grind it, cook it *yourself*.

(This is a general principle, not a hard-and-fast rule. It's good to splurge occasionally.)

Some people take this to extremes, *growing* their own food. Farming and chicken-rearing may be fun, but they take up time, so you don't need to go all the way. Just adopt the make-it-yourself mantra, most of the time, and you'll sustain your body effectively.

There's nothing else you need to know about food.

Focus on sleep

Too many people neglect sleep. But it's part of health, no less vital than food or exercise. So put in the same effort. Good sleep takes a bit of hard work.

The basics: find your body's natural sleep rhythm—whether you're a lark or an owl—and go to bed and get up at the same times every day, as often as practical. Most people need 7-8 quiet hours, minimum. You're probably *not* one of the freaks who doesn't.

So put down the iPad and phone; the blue tones in their screens fool your body into thinking it's morning. (Kindles are ok, but take it easy on volume.) Meditate. But whatever works for you, get your sleep.

Stand up straight

Bad posture is a modern curse. (The younger generation has it even worse, with "text neck".) Every 2.5cm you hold your head forward **doubles** the strain on your spine. Western cities are full of Quasimodos.

So if you do nothing else for your health, **sit and stand up straight**.

The best mental model centres on the **shoulders**. When standing, imagine a) your head is balanced on your shoulders rather than fixed there, so you have to keep it in place; and b) the rest of your body is hanging down from your shoulders, rather than holding them up from below.

Here's an exercise. Pull yourself up to maximum

height, straightening your spine and neck. Now relax back down . . . *halfway.*

You'll still be straighter than normal, but can hold it much longer. Walk around holding this position. In time, it'll become your new (and better) normal.

You'll find yourself breathing easier, keeping fitter, feeling more confident in your dealings with others. And zero back problems.

Now for the rest of fitness.

STAYING IN SHAPE

Mens sana in corpore sano. A healthy mind in a healthy body. Yes, the next step after stress, food, and sleep is *exercise*.

First up: your body evolved to *move*. Not peer at a screen. Or sit on a sofa. In fact, most First World health issues are the result of chasing *comfort* rather than *health*.

Hot showers, soft mattresses, and upright chairs aren't actually much good for you. So recognise this, and take action to keep your body functional.

Fortunately, fitness is simple. It's ==some sort of push, some sort of pull, and some sort of squat==.

A "push" is anything that works your front and

triceps, like a pushup. A "pull" is anything that works your back and biceps, like a pullup. While a "squat" is, well, a squat. (It works your legs and bum.)

Working on pushes, pulls, and squats, from slow and grinding moves to fast and explosive ones, build the three things that matter for a balance of strength, endurance, and power: core, cardio, and grip.

Staying in shape is a learnable skill; these are the exam criteria.

Your **core** muscles are the lats (big fan-shaped one on your back) glutes (big meaty ones in your bum) and obliques (sides of your torso.) In a world where few jobs involve lifting big weights, many people don't even *use* their lats and glutes—they are "inactive". Which is the whole problem.

Without the lats, glutes, and obliques, moving your body falls to smaller muscles not made for the job. And this is the source of those all-too-common ailments: back pain, neck ache, bad posture.

(You're sitting up straight already, right?)

Cardio health involves your heart. Pumping blood is how oxygen and nutrients get around the body; an unfit heart doesn't make its deliveries on time. Which means your flesh and bones don't get fed.

If it makes your heart work harder, it's cardio. Swimming, cycling, running, and a skipping rope all work great, but you don't need equipment or space. Just move a bit faster, a bit more explosively. Get that heart pumping.

Last, your **hands** are second only to your **head** as

tools for reaching your goals—meaning a strong **grip** pays back big. The human animal was born to hang; it's another basic skill many have lost. Don't be among them.

There are many activities that'll give you those pushes, pulls, and squats and build your core, cardio, and grip strength. Some tried-and-tested options include **calisthenics**, **kettlebells**, and **Yoga**. Let's look at each.

Do calisthenics

There's all sorts of jargon in fitness, like internal and external rotation, closed-chain and open-chain movements, reps and sets. Learn it if you want; it's useful.

But the most useful concept of all is *progression*. As in *progressive calisthenics* (it means "beautiful strength"). It's a workout discipline going back to the ancient Greeks.

Progression means you start simple and level up. If you can't do a pushup on the floor, do one against the wall. Then do two. Then ten. Then *sets*. Once you can do three sets of 50, level up and do pushups against a table instead. When you feel ready, hit the floor.

As you get stronger, it gets easier. When it gets easier, make it harder. That's all it is, really.

Classic calisthenics moves are the pushup, pullup, squat, leg raise, back bridge, and handstand. Each has a simple move to start with; each has a "master move" to aim for. The point is to level up *in tune with what your body can handle*. Joints and tendons adapt slower than muscle; stepping up over time gives all the bits a chance to keep up.

Progressive calisthenics builds the body that's right, at the rate that's right. And there's always somewhere to start, whether you're 20 or 70.

Work out with weights

You build muscle by forcing it to act against resistance. Your body doesn't care whether that's bodyweight or barbells; resistance is resistance. But while calisthenics increases **proprioception**—awareness of your body in space—it's also useful to build experience of moving things that *aren't* your body, around you.

For the latter, try **kettlebells**.

Any free weights work. But these cannonballs-with-a-handle, deliberately unwieldy and unbalanced, get results fast. They're also *fun*. You can dual-wield 'em, hold them in odd orientations, even juggle with them. (In time.)

Kettlebells range from a tiny 4kg to 48kg and beyond. Few men can press even a 24kg above their head. Most men start with a 16, most women with a 12, but with practice the sky's the limit.

The basic moves are the swing, the squat, and the get-up. Just a few days learning them can set you up for a lifetime of strength and health.

Train your grip

You have almost no muscle in your hands. Your grip comes from your forearms, upper arms, lats, right down your back—which is why **grip strength** is such a terrific indicator of health.

A strong grip keeps you functional throughout life. (It's the last thing to go when you get old.) It also correlates with mortality: each 5kg increase in grip strength matches to a 15% lower chance of dying. (It's more accurate than heart health.) In other words, if you can grip twice the 44kg or so of Mr Average—which isn't hard to train for—you're three-quarters less likely to kick the bucket this year.

Both calisthenics and kettlebells train grip big-time.

(In prog cali, it's hanging from a bar and doing pushups on the pads of your fingers; in kettlebells it's wrapping your hands around handles.)

What better way of doing life is there than an activity that unequivocally increases your healthy *lifespan*?

The metric works because a strong grip is an *outcome* of balanced health across your entire upper body. Which means greater core stability and strength. However you train, adopt grip as a useful measure—for the whole of your life.

(Plank, hollow, and twist)

If a training schedule is truly beyond you, at least do *something* that keeps those lats, glutes, and obliques functional. The ==plank, hollow body, and spine twist== are a worthwhile minimum, taking minutes a day.

To **plank**, lie on your front and prop yourself on your elbows, upper arms vertical and forearms out flat on the floor. Straighten your legs and back and neck into a solid line. And **hold it there**.

Then plank on each **side**. Lie on one side, raise yourself on one elbow—upper arm vertical as before—and hold, keeping your body straight again. Hold the other arm straight up if you like.

With the plank, the **hollow body** is the other move in

Gymnastics 101. Lie on your back and **flatten your spine** against the floor. When you can keep it there without strain, **raise your legs** off the floor to add resistance.

Next is the **spine twist**. Sit on the floor. Without straining or moving your legs, and keeping your spine vertical, **turn to look behind you**. And hold it there.

For any of these, one minute is good. Two, excellent. Beyond that, awesome.

And if that's all you ever do, you're doing life okay.

Think Yoga

Calisthenics and kettlebells are about *moving* your body; Yoga and meditation are about keeping it *still*.

Why does this matter? Because quieting the body creates a sense of inner calm and peace. Which is great for health. (Live in the now, remember?)

There are a thousand variants of the ancient Indian pastime. Some focus on its monastic origins, most are more like workouts, without all the Omming. Test a few and feel how they meld mind and body as one.

This quartet—do calisthenics, lift kettlebells, train grip, think Yoga—is all you need to attain the supreme healthy strength and fitness of the ancients.

Namaste.

(And learn to fight)

No macho bullshit here: the best fight, always, is the one you never have.

But being *able* to fight gives you poise and confidence beyond belief, even when your goal is to never use it. There's no greater affirmation of the ability to do life than feeling ready to take on another human being in hand-to-hand combat.

So as a test of your movement and resistance training, round out your plan for your body with a few sparring and grappling sessions a month.

A human instructor is best at first. Learn the basic stances, how to punch and kick, get the upper hand when on the floor. See how to block with a stick and defend against a blade. Later, you can maintain your practice with a punchbag and martial arts dummy.

You'll never need to use them . . . hopefully. But you'll never forget they're there.

That's your body built, ready for (almost) anything. These activities will build the strongest base layer of Maslow's Pyramid possible.

Now let's look to the second layer. But first . . .

... DEALING WITH AGING

We all get old. This is unfortunate.

While there *are* creatures that don't die of decrepitude, and science will one day let us join them, for now we're all dead men walking.

But until your day comes, time's effects can be mitigated. The catchphrase: *don't chase youth, chase health.*

(From Charles Eugster, who competed in athletics until his death at 97.)

Youthful vigour doesn't come from makeup or plastic surgery. It comes from *within*. Attitude, aptitude, a positive outlook.

In fact, an energetic old age is the triumphant last

chapter of a life successfully done.

When good exercise is keeping the blood flowing through your body . . . when active thinking is driving connections between your neurons . . . when flow states are keeping you happy and connected to your work and the people around you . . . it's then you have the best chance of living a long, healthy life.

Chase health, not youth. Always.

With that last thought on the body, it's time to build your **intellect**.

NURTURE YOUR INTELLECT

The base of Maslow's Pyramid might be termed the **body layer**: food, water, sleep, the things you need to make it to the next full moon. The next layer up—**safety**—is where you start looking at life on a longer timescale. Owning property, investing for the future, building up a stake in society.

For those interested in doing life, this is where the fun starts. Because, of course, it uses your **mind**.

There's an old argument about whether intelligence comes from nature or nurture. The answer's obvious when you consider we're all born with the same lump of grey matter in our heads. We all have the same flock of neurons (around 100bn) each one capable of the same number of synaptic connections (up to 10,000). So nature is just the baseline. *Nurture* is what matters.

What you take in through your senses, the connections you make with people, the subjects you study, the thoughts you think and emotions you feel—*this* is personal growth. Everything that makes you "you" is the result of nurturing.

Of course, a lot of this happens in your early years. And that means some people reach adulthood with a head start. (Tip: choose your parents carefully.)

But here's the upside: your brain continues making new connections throughout life. So it's *never* too late to build a better one. The nurturing of your intellect from early adulthood on depends on *you*.

If you're reading one good book a week and doing

stuff to find your flow, you're building up the practices of successful living already. But what many intelligent adults *lack* are the **mental models** to turn their lives towards maximum advantage in their pursuit of value.

Your mind is a superpowerful, superconnected supercomputer for living your best life.

But it needs effective applications to function.

So to nurture your mind, make sure you know what those apps are.

Call 'em **how to learn**, **how to think**, and **how to act**.

HOW TO LEARN

Remember how much of school was about learning by rote? That's why you haven't used it since.

Learning is not about memorising rote facts. It's about developing *tools for thinking*. Thinking is what schools should teach—not who Henry VIII divorced or decapitated.

(This has a bearing on how your *kids* do life, of course. Don't worry, some tips on that later.)

Most people's minds are so clogged with useless *whats* that they have trouble with *whys*. Luckily, it's never too late to start your education.

First up: **we learn the way our brains learn.** (Because we *are* our brains.)

However you take in information—eyes, ears, fingertips—it all becomes the same stuff: electrical impulses spackled across your brain. These spackles cause neurons to fire at synapses, which then excite other neurons, and so on. You are a mass of overlapping, interlocking networks in your head.

Repeating stimuli cause these networks ("schema") to strengthen, becoming persistent patterns such as memories or behaviours. Similar stimuli produce similar patterns, which is why you first understand a thing in terms of other things like it.

And that's the key to effective learning. To integrate areas of knowledge and see them as *parts of a whole*, the way our brains do. *Not* disassociated lists of facts.

==Learning is a process of integration==.

This is why school didn't work for you. Schools like to *divide*, subjects in silos. Were you ever taught Egypt's rise was about economics, not art? Or how Newton and Maxwell's successes shaped the Industrial Revolution? Bet not. But they're connected nonetheless, like the schema in your brain.

To integrate knowledge effectively, some learnings are better than others. Let's call them **skill** subjects and **knowledge** subjects. The former help you perform tasks; the latter let you make effective decisions.

The skills subjects are the basics: reading, writing, and arithmetic. The knowledge subjects are history, mathematics, physics, and literature. Studying them is the route to a completely educated mind, capable of learning anything *else* . . . in depth.

A-grade your three R's

Sort of obvious this, but it bears repeating: ==make sure the basics are up to scratch==. Reading, writing, and 'rithmetic are not subjects, but **general skills** underlying every area of a successful life.

Reading comes from, well, you guessed it. Read widely and everywhere; your reading speed will rise with volume, and your ability to make sense of a book will rise by selecting good ones. A **Kindle** is your best friend; all the Great Works are free.

Writing is how you make sense to others and function in the world: it's how you organise information logically and sequentially. Bad writing is bad thinking—and many people write *appallingly*. To practice, write summaries and notes on everything you read and do; your writing will soon improve.

Arithmetic, or basic numeracy, is rarer than it should be. Practice how to add and divide in your head; don't let positives and negatives, powers, fractions, and the magic of compound interest fool you. Numbers are how you get a grip on the world.

The three basic skills instil *intellectual rigour*. (To practice, get hold of the GMAT questions commonly used by business schools as entry criteria; they test all three.) They force you to be self-critical, and review and revise constantly.

But whatever your goals, **get the basics in place**.

Get into maths

Mathematics (a separate subject to basic numeracy) is the ultimate integration: the whole of reality reduced to x's and y's. That's why it's among the four subjects worth studying as a base to whatever *other* stuff you want to learn: it's wholly **conceptual**.

While divided into pure and applied, the main use of mathematics in doing life is to help you understand *how nature works*. Of course, it's a vast subject, so let's cut it down to size. The three basic areas to study are **algebra**, **geometry**, and **trigonometry**, which lead you to the level-up that matters: **calculus**.

Algebra comes first for its use of notation: the basic method of generalising and abstracting instances into methods. While the diagrams of **geometry** help you relate it to reality, as Euclid discovered millennia ago. **Trigonometry**, of course, completes the triangle, by relating these concepts to each other.

(And the better your mind gets at relating concepts to each other, the more deeply you'll understand the world.)

But this trio is most useful as a base for jumping into **calculus**, the basis of much technology and engineering. Relax: it's nowhere near as hard as people imagine. Calculus is at root a case study in integration and differentiation. These are the most important concepts not just for learning, but for thinking.

Practicing maths problems will also help you study **formal logic**—a skill for making decisions—later.

There's one more reason to study mathematics: the people. Human stories behind these discoveries add depth and colour to your understanding. So learn who Euclid, Euler, Gauss, Riemann, and Hilbert were, and how they came to eurekas. Mathematics is not some frozen berg of known knowns; it's a living field, with new applications being discovered all the time.

These areas will open your mind to far more complex ones, like the octonions that may explain reality itself. Don't be scared of maths.

Know your history

To do life, history is one of the four essential areas to study. Because it shows you what people actually *did*.

Written history, of course, has biases, so read broadly and from a range of viewpoints. History didn't start with the Romans. For most of civilisation the world's axis was Asia, not the West; today's Middle East wasn't always like that; how wars really start and how nations always act zero-sum, preferring a small win-lose even if there's a huge win-win to be had. The truth is startling.

By integrating your knowledge of the past you'll see how every civilisation follows the same cycle: first a lawless free-for-all, then government and regulation, then welfare and entitlements, then unsustainable bloat and collapse. How names and faces change with time—but people's motivations don't. It's a study of principles, revealing the basic factors shaping human development and the effects of ideas on societies.

A critical knowledge of macroeconomics and geopolitics—history—is a rulebook for how the world actually works. Done right, history is the whole of the humanities, in the same way physics is the whole of science.

Study history not to learn about the past, but to understand the present.

Work out physics

Science—the understanding of nature—isn't really a subject. It's a *method*. And its core is **physics**, the third of your four "knowledge" areas.

Some say it's the hardest part of science. Well, certainly it's the deepest. But go in with the right attitude—evidence-based, logic-driven, there is no supernatural and A is always A, not B—and you'll be fine. More, you'll learn what physics really is: a *romantic* subject, full of truth and beauty.

Once you learn it's the electron orbits of H_2O that make every snowflake unique . . . that every speck of gold in your wedding band was forged in the heart of the sun . . . that the laws governing a fallen apple are the same laws governing how planets form around faraway stars . . . you'll realise what physics adds to life. It's the Big Questions: how the Universe began, how life got started, how consciousness works. (Even if it doesn't have all the big *answers* yet.)

Physics is fundamentally about finding the *simplicity* behind nature's complexity. So let's get simple: the unifying theme of physics is the ==field equation==. Understand what a field equation is, and you'll half-understand anything a physicist says. (Which is more than a fair few actual physicists will.)

Formal definition: *a field equation is a partial differential equation that determines the time evolution and spatial orientation of a physical field, like magnetism or gravity.*

In simpler terms: a field equation describes how *dynamic things behave over time.*

Recall how iron filings make patterns over a magnet, understand those patterns can be represented as algebraic notation, and you've got the concept.

Newton's and Einstein's field equations explain gravity. Faraday's and Maxwell's, electromagnetism. Schrödinger's define quantum mechanics; two guys named Yang and Mills came up with those for the forces holding atoms together. And the as-yet-incomplete ones unifying the four fundamental forces of nature—the "theory of everything"—will be field equations too.

Three other fundamental bits matter. The **periodic table**, the **electromagnetic spectrum**, and the

Standard Model.

The **periodic table** is a list of elements ordered by each element's atomic number. (The number of protons in its nucleus.) Elements with similar atomic structures have similar properties; the table shows how they relate. Get to know it.

The **electromagnetic spectrum** brings together everything that has a wavelength and frequency in one diagram—from the radio waves bringing you mobile broadband to the high-energy gamma radiation that'll kill you after a mushroom cloud does its thing. Waves, like field equations, are everywhere in physics, and the two are deeply intertwined.

Because atoms are made of smaller bits—a nucleus of protons and neutrons, with electrons whizzing around them—one more table rounds out the basics. The **Standard Model** is a list of particles that make up atoms, both the everyday "nucleons" (like protons and neutrons) and exotics that only exist for an instant. It's not complete yet, but it is very, very accurate.

Like mathematics, history, and writing, physics will hone your mind. You'll get in the habit of looking for evidence, stop jumping to conclusions, and exercise critical judgement at every juncture, in accordance with the scientific method.

That's the beauty of physics.

Love literature

If history is the whole of the humanities and physics is the whole of science, **literature** is the whole of the arts. It's a Great Conversation between thinking people down the centuries; studying literature is your ticket to the party.

Literature is separate to the skill of writing. It's the sum total of humanity's creative output in language: epics, novels, plays, and poems. And that means *worldwide*.

On a global scale, the Ramayana and Mahabharata, the four great novels of ancient China, the Homeric sagas matter more than Shakespeare and Dickens. (Although those guys are good, too.) Learn to read them (even in translation) and learn the differences between literary traditions that define cultures.

Literature is more than art: it showcases people's view of themselves in relation to others at a certain point in time. It's the comments thread of history, and will help you integrate concepts about Man's place in the Universe—i.e. philosophy—better than any dry textbook on metaphysics or epistemology ever could.

That's the quartet of subjects to learn: mathematics, history, physics, and literature. And once you've got started, it's time to challenge accepted wisdom on something else: how to *think*.

HOW TO THINK

Together, these seven areas of learning—the three R's, mathematics, history, physics, and literature—give you the building blocks of something even more important: *thinking*.

All education should be about teaching how to think. (Very little is.)

Thinking is how you bring your S2 to the fore in every situation that could be bettered by it is how you engage with civility, argue from evidence, and make decisions with confidence.

So learning right leads to thinking right. The main parts of thinking well are knowing how to apply **logic**, recognise people's **biases**, and understand **risk**.

(Learn logic)

Much pain stems from **contradictions**: feeling conflicted about situations and choices. So doing life needs a method of resolving them.

That's why the last part of nurturing your intellect—an eighth skill that puts the first seven to work—is ==formal logic==. A means of determining *whether something is so.* (Or at least knowable.)

Formal logic is where mathematics and philosophy meet: assertions and arguments written down like equations, so you can check if their *form* is valid without linguistic goo and dribble getting in the way. Aristotle's syllogisms (*all men are mortal; Socrates is a man; therefore, Socrates is mortal*) are one formal logic. Computing's "operators" (IF x AND y THEN z) are another. Once you reduce a belief to its underlying form, deciding truth is easy. A is A; it is not B.

(And politicians wouldn't be able to *claim* A is B, if they had to prove it logically. Although parliamentary debates wouldn't be much fun.)

Defining problems in logical form, constructing proofs and testing hypotheses; *this* is how you master the ability to think critically and make rational decisions based on valid inferences. To *reason*.

That's why logic is separate to your three basic skills and four subject areas for doing life. All learning is a process of integration: finding common denominators that unite different things. Logic is a process of *differentiation*: seeing the critical divisions between things that let you make sound judgements.

Logic is the apex skill of thinking, the spice that makes knowledge worth consuming. The Russian-American philosopher Ayn Rand summed it up best: "We must *know*! We may not simply *believe*!"

Where to start? Read up on syllogisms, then IF—THEN—ELSE operators, then Boolean algebra (AND, OR, XOR, NOT.) That's ninety percent right there. As a bonus, when you can write down situations in logical form you'll learn to recognise **fallacies**.

Life has no contradictions. If you find any, check your premises, because one or more will be wrong. Logic is how you do it.

(Understand biases)

Kahnemann (of S1/S2 fame) also came up with **cognitive biases**, the behaviours our unthinking S1 pushes us into.

If you want to think critically and act logically, cognitive biases matter, because they're the source of *illogical* behaviour. When you act from your heart or gut, rather than by inductive reasoning (looking at evidence) or deductive logic (thinking it through).

Being ==guided by your S2, rather than pushed by your S1==, is a key skill for doing life.

So now you're equipped with the apex S2 skill—**formal logic**—apply it to recognising when cognitive biases are in play, so you can neuter them when needed. It's hard, but the payoff is huge.

There are hundreds of cognitive biases, but a few matter most. Once you understand the principle, you'll see others everywhere.

The biggie is **Loss Aversion**. People put more value on not losing what they already have than on making a bigger gain. It's why people spend an hour searching for a lost £10 note when they could have earned £20 working instead. Turn down a job with prospects because they'll lose their welfare benefits. Stay in a bad relationship even if a better one beckons.

(Loss Aversion also explains stockmarket investing in full. Successful investors cut their losses early and ride their winners longer. Losers in thrall to Loss Aversion do the opposite.)

See how toxic cognitive biases are?

Four others control most daily life for most people, dubbed availability, familiarity, and confirmation biases. (The Dunning-Kruger Effect has its own section, up next.) To see them in action, look at any tabloid newspaper or its online equivalent.

Availability Bias rears up when you use information that's easy to get hold of, rather than represents the actual situation. We all do it—but what's close at hand is rarely the big picture. If your data was cheap, it's probably incomplete.

Familiarity Bias takes charge when you stick to what you know, even if greater payback is available elsewhere. You're mistaking the comfort of home for the opportunities of the world. For greater gains, get out there and explore.

While **Confirmation Bias** is rampant in public and private debate: it's the tendency to see new information as backing up what you already believe, instead of challenging it.

See what all these have in common? You're **thinking small**. Basing your actions on your narrow personal experience, rather than the broader world out there. And that world's too interesting to ignore.

(Manage risk)

Successful living is risk management. You run more risk of death crossing a city street than flying 10,000km in a plane, yet thanks to cognitive biases more people are scared of planes than traffic.

The media uses this expertly. Every story zooms in a a ruinous but rare what-if of a broad government policy; every lawsuit focusses on a small risk rather than the larger advantage.

==Risk is not a reason not to do stuff==.

Risk management helps you understand the *return* from doing stuff. Get a sensible perspective on it.

The **Dunning-Kruger Effect**, up next, will help.

HOW TO ACT

The next step after making a decision is taking *effective action.* Taking effective action is hard, due to the **Dunning-Kruger Effect**.

The Dunning-Kruger Effect is another cognitive bias, rooted in our S1 and making us act on instinct. Dunning-Kruger is in play when people think they're better than they are. Perversely, the less competent they are, the greater their tendency to think they're at the top of their game.

The Dunning-Kruger Effect is common, afflicting six out of ten people.

So to take effective action, you first need to ask yourself: am I *competent*?

There's a tool for that, sometimes called the **Four Stages of Teaching** or the **Learning Matrix**.

unconsciously incompetent	unconsciously competent
consciously incompetent	consciously competent

Dunning-Kruger is rife in the first box: you don't know what you don't know, or *unconscious of your incompetence*. Get out of this box, fast, by learning something about the subject.

You start beating the bias in the next box, *conscious incompetence*. You still don't know, but you *know* you don't know. Which sets the scene for personal growth.

Third box is where you start delivering. You can do it, and you know you can do it—*consciously competent*. But you're not an expert yet.

The last box is the state of **flow** you've already met: *unconsciously competent*. Your ability is up to the task and you know how to get even better.

To ensure your actions are effective, check the box.

DO UNTO OTHERS

Understanding Dunning-Kruger also gives you the ideal way to deal with people: ==treat others how you'd like to be treated yourself==. Yes, it's that simple.

Because being aware of what you don't know solves a problem in ethics. Indeed, the *central* problem.

(Ethics—basically, right and wrong—is a branch of philosophy, alongside metaphysics (the nature of things) epistemology (how knowledge is created) logic (reasoning and decisions) politics (how society is organised) and aesthetics (art and beauty). See how these sync with skills and subjects worth learning?)

The **Trolley Problem** puts you on a railway bridge. Below, a runaway train is about to hit five people. You can divert it onto a branch line . . . where it will kill *one* person. **Would you pull the lever?**

90% say yes. And that's where the fun starts.

Because you should *not*.

Mr Todd was just out for a walk near the branch line, minding his own business, and *you killed him*.

Not very "do unto others", is it? And there's the rub. ==The greatest good for the greatest number involves infringing on the rights of others.==

This is where Big Government, bad policy, and restrictions on freedom all start: strangers thinking it's okay to take decisions about your life.

You let your S1 take control, and it turned you into a murderer. If you doubt that, rephrase the problem. What if, instead of pulling a lever, you've got to *push someone onto the track*? Same dilemma. Yet now 80% say they *wouldn't* do it. The more it feels like murder, the fewer take the plunge. (Luckily for Mr Todd.)

How about *three* people at risk? Net savings drop from four to two. Or just *one* . . . but it's a young woman with a bright future, versus a doddering old-timer?

Try *two hundred* people on the main line . . . and 196 on the branch. Same net saving. And now you're among history's most notorious mass murderers.

Is it right to inhibit one person's life if it makes a better life for others? No. It isn't. So don't let your $S1$ take decisions for you. Do unto others.

POLITICS AND ECONOMICS

Most of us live under laws. Most of us exchange value using money. Therefore any successful life-liver needs to understand two societal forces: **politics** and **economics**.

Politics is how you think society should be organised: rights, freedoms, responsibilities. Economics is how society uses resources: producing, distributing, consuming. Meaning they're linked. As you'll see, each is half the other.

Politics first, and why it isn't a linear Left-Right axis, but a two-dimensional landscape.

Understand your politics

Many people are frustrated by politics. Because too often, it tries to put you on a one-dimensional axis: Left or Right? And you're not one-dimensional.

The good news: nor is politics.

In fact, politics has *two* dimensions, with different axes for *social* and *economic* freedoms. A diagram that brings these together is the **Nolan Chart**, whose four corners represent the extremes of political leanings.

Many people only half-identify with traditional Left or Right. So if you place yourself and your preferred political party on the Nolan Chart, you'll probably find you're further apart than you thought. And a large part of the population isn't catered to at all. Try it and see.

This is where most books might state there is "no wrong answer". That there is a diverse range of views and no one is more correct than any other.

Unfortunately, this is wrong.

There *is* a "correct" political leaning that accords with doing life successfully—and only one. (*If* you accept the rationale for life's meaning at the start of this book.) It's called **libertarianism**.

For those who've heard of it at all (it's rare outside the USA) the word conjures images of gun-toting ranchers and tinfoil-hatted extremists in places like Montana and Nevada. Yes, it has its extremists, like any other ideology. But let's use the Nolan Chart to see why libertarianism isn't scary at all.

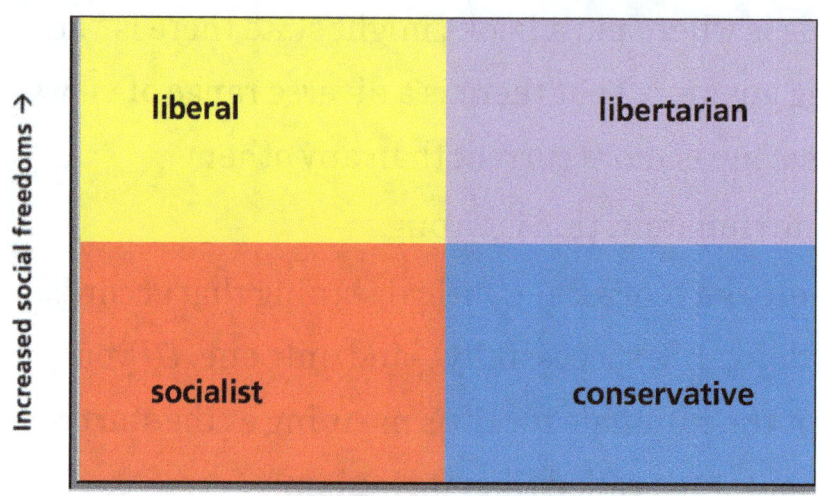

If you believe people need to be constrained and corralled, you're low on social freedoms. But that alone doesn't make you "left wing"; authoritarians can lean left *or* right. (The red and blue boxes.) Conservatism, notionally embracing business and enterprise (high economic freedom) also tends authoritarian when it comes to your private life; its extreme at bottom right is fascism. "The left" spans a spectrum of views on how people should live their lives, from North Korea to San Francisco. (The red and yellow boxes.) It's only if you're big on wealth redistribution and equality of outcome (low economic freedoms) that you're truly a socialist, whose bottom-left extreme is communism. (Zero social *and* economic freedom, comrades!)

The yellow box, liberalism, believes in high social freedoms: equal individual rights under the law for all. A good (nay, *great*) thing. But today's liberals, mostly, aren't big on the classical liberalism of John Stuart Mill, falling short on economic freedoms: a fondness for punitive taxes and wealth redistribution. Putting them on the Left.

That leaves libertarianism: high social freedoms *and* high economic ones. As a check, drill into your *own* views for a moment.

Do you think the law should apply to all, equally? That your life and how you live it is your choice, not your government's? That being black, gay, or female should not affect your basic rights? (All high social freedoms.) That you have the right to start a business and strive for profit; that competition and innovation are positive forces; that governments play too big a role in the economy? (All high economic ones.)

If so, you lean libertarian. Up to 27% of people do without realising. (If that sounds low, recall most elected governments win with barely 30% of the vote.)

Doing life—in this little book's philosophy—is a self-actualised endeavour, using your intellect and abilities to pursue your goals. To do that, you need high social *and* high economic freedoms. That's libertarianism.

Because conservatism, socialism, and liberalism all lead to Big Government, a vast state with huge powers over your life. And maximising your opportunities needs *small* government. One focussed on protecting your rights as an individual—and nothing else.

Equal rights for all under the law, no discrimination based on race or sex, zero coercion in your relations with others, government that stays out of your way, and nonviolence except in self-defence. Sounds good? That's libertarianism.

Let's look at economics. There's a right and wrong answer there, too.

Understand the economy

If politics is how *society* is organised, economics is how *resources* are organised. Since most of history is about control over resources—land, gold, oil—economics is the other half of history.

As with politics, there is a right and wrong way to "do" economics. The right way—the one that best accords with life as a self-actualised individual—is decided by the principle of **comparative advantage**.

In today's economy, you don't need land, gold, or oil to pursue your goals. Because you have resources of your *own* to exchange for value: your intellect and abilities. So to maximise your return, you'll want to do what you're best at (since customers will pay more for a job done well than a job done badly) and buy in what you're not.

This is the law of comparative advantage, sometimes called "the magic of trade". Comparative advantage is the basis of the only economic system that works, providing ever-greater opportunities to people while producing ever-better products and services to customers: **free-market capitalism**.

In this ideal System of the World, companies compete and innovate to offer goods and services customers want, with profit as their incentive to work hard and get better. Supply is matched to demand by the price mechanism; companies win or lose depending on how well they satisfy people's Wants.

(Wants. Not "Needs". The most evil sentence ever

written is "From each according to his ability; to each according to his need." No reason to work harder or smarter, because all your energies go on someone else's "need". The definition of serfdom: being compelled for work for another's goals.)

True, capitalism does not create an "equal" society. That's not its point. And no system ever does. (For "equality", try North Korea.) Why would you want to be the same as everyone else, anyway? That's not life.

It's not perfect, obvs. No system ever is. Management guru Peter Drucker: *"It does not work too well, but nothing else works at all."*

However, it *is* why we have kick-ass cars, amazing software applications, fast air travel, awesome mobile phones, access to capital. All the good stuff.

And thanks to competition driven by the profit motive, the best gets cheaper and better, every year.

That's all the economy is: people buying and selling stuff to each other with cash and credit. (For a visual primer, look up investor Ray Dalio's short video, "How the Economic Machine Works".)

There are only three other things you need to know to understand the whole of it. The **short-term debt cycle** (basically, the time between recessions) the **long-term debt cycle** (between wars) and the **productivity growth curve** (how fast you get better at stuff).

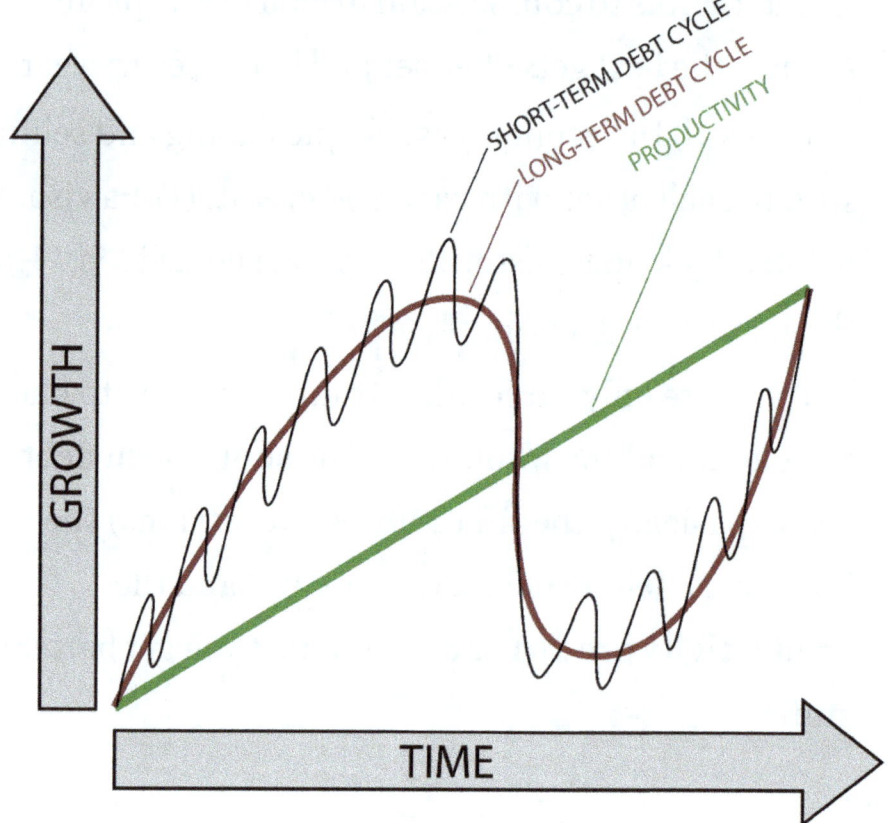

The **productivity growth curve** is what matters to doing life successfully: people doing a) what they're good at, and b) paying others to do everything else. It's the single factor that contributes to rising living standards over time. And it's the one under your control. *You* get to choose how productive you are, by honing your intellect and improving the products and services you offer. (Whether you do it on your own or as part of a team, such as a company.)

Two other factors *aren't* under your control.

The **short-term debt cycle** is boom and bust. In good times, with high demand, banks make more credit available cheaply to those who can satisfy it. In time, supply overtakes demand, prices fall, credit tightens, and the economy goes into recession.

You can't do anything about this. But understanding it will help you ride the cycle. Except at the end of a long-term debt cycle, the high point of each short-term debt cycle is higher than the high point of the previous one. Meaning that despite blips and burps, everything's getting better over time.

The **long-term debt cycle**—every 60-80 years—is a bigger deal. A major shift in the economy, caused by debt burdens getting too big for even banks to sustain. Not a recession, but a *depression*. Then assets are sold at firesale prices, innovators see opportunities, and the cycle begins afresh. (And often society with it.)

Free-market capitalism is how you do life best. Just remember: **productivity** above all.

A WORD ON WEALTH

With economics explained, this little guide to health, wealth, and happiness doesn't have much else to say about money. Because money is a side effect.

Yes, you should live within your means, earn your own money, ask no charity, and invest for your future. That's part of moving towards what you value.

But ==wealth is not about money==. Life isn't about making a killing. It's about making a *living*.

If you have a ton of gold in your hut, but the hut's in the middle of the Sahara with nary a cockroach for 1000km, are you "rich"?

In our superabundant society, wealth is *access to goods and services*. Stuff you can *use* to create and exchange value. And thanks to our great force for good—**free-market capitalism**—we've got one helluva lot of that.

If you live in a capitalist society—even on the bottom rung—you are very, very lucky. Because authoritarians don't have *total* control over your life—which means you have a greater opportunity to move towards what you value.

So understand that capitalism is not out to get you. It's there to *serve* you. It's a positive force for good.

Be a capitalist. You never see a happy socialist, do you?

MAKING MONEY

While money isn't wealth, most would agree it's nice to *have* money. All that root-of-all-evil stuff? Nonsense. Money is *great*.

Money is great because it lets us agree a value for any product or service, based on how good it is and how many people want it. That's why money is the token of exchange between billions of people, spanning borders, cultures, and creeds.

On the ancient Silk Roads, silver coins from Rome settled debts across Asia. One tribe struck coins with its own kings on one side and Chinese characters on the other. In parts of Brazil, pieces of eight from the pirate era are *still used*.

That's all a capitalist economy is—individuals with different needs and wants, buying and selling products and services with cash and credit. It's living proof that life is about moving towards value, and that you can obtain value by trading with others.

This makes *earning* money a simple matter. ==The better you are at delivering a product or service to the people who want it, the more you'll earn.==

Note this principle doesn't cover inherited money, gambling wins, or picking stocks. It's about money paid for work performed—in other words, the sort of work most of us do. So given Power Laws, following it *won't* get you into that club of eight at the top.

But you don't do envy any more, do you? And it *can* get you into the top 1% of earners, with a great work/life balance to boot.

An annual income of **£100,000+**, enough for anyone to live sustainably and invest for the future sensibly, is an option for anyone who wants it. All you need is a saleable skill, and customers to sell it to. And *every* normally-abled adult can develop one of those, just by doing life successfully.

There's even an instruction manual. Reaching a six-figure income takes just 100 days of focussed effort, with actual tasks and checklists to follow each day. See 100days100grand.com.

UNDERSTANDING PEOPLE

Up now to the third layer of Maslow, **belonging**. Where you work on your relationships with others.

People are strange. But they can be understood. Mars and Venus, Myers-Briggs, the OCEAN model: they all help. But to understand where other people are coming from, all you really need is one question: ==how do you respond to expectations?==

(Expectations span both those you have of yourself—"inner expectations"—and those others have of you, or "outer expectations".)

Everyone is somewhere on this diagram by author Gretchen Rubin.

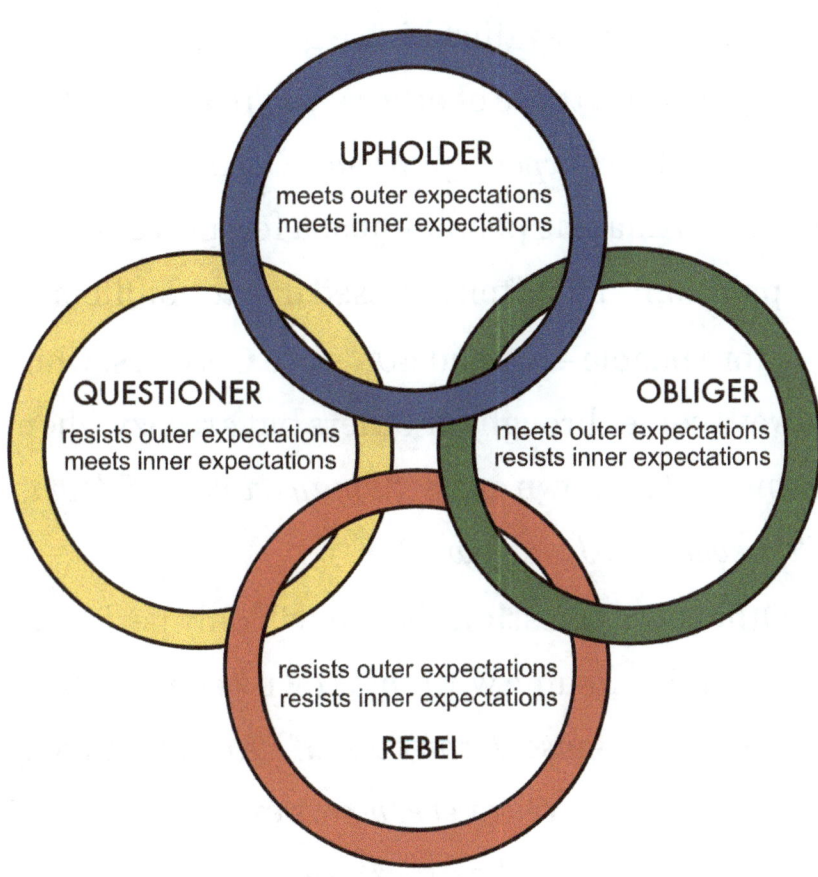

If you deliver against high expectations of both your own goals and those of others, you're an **Upholder**. "*I do what others expect of me—and what I expect from myself.*" Amazing people—just a few percent of the population—but often stressed due to conflicts.

More people—around 40%—are **Obligers**, who always come through for others but are lazy when it comes to their own goals. "*I may let myself down, but I'll never let others down.*"

Others are **Questioners**—they'll only perform for others if it's in tune with their own beliefs. ("*If it doesn't make sense, I won't do it.*") And an unlucky few are **Rebels**, who resist *everyone's* expectations. ("*You can't make me—and neither can I.*")

Once you know someone's type, you can behave in a

way that make the most of it. For instance, **Obligers** often declare their private goals in public, or book hard deadlines, so they'll be letting someone down if they fail; that's their motivator. **Questioners** react better when the benefits and outcomes are explained to them. And so on.

How do you respond to expectations? This $64,000 Question is equivalent to the Ultimate Question in marketing, "Would you recommend us to friends and family?" Or the £100,000 Question in freelancing, "What does success look like?"

Use it to understand everyone you meet.

UNDERSTANDING ORGANISATIONS

Everyone's experienced bad organisations: government agencies, indifferent banks, appalling customer service. Even when the people within it were genuinely good folk. The reason—and the key to understanding **organisations**—is that ==structure creates culture==.

People act according to the incentives on offer. If the Call Centre's reward metric is handling time per call, expect to be treated brusquely by the agent. If a car salesman earns more commission from high-interest financing than selling cars, expect to be pushed towards a pricey credit deal. In a famine, expect good people to do *very* bad things for the last mouldy loaf.

Structures, overt or evolved, define how people behave. Often, they have no choice in the matter. Understand this, and you'll see how otherwise decent people can behave badly towards you: they're trapped by circumstance and can't do anything else without it costing them dearly.

And maybe, knowing this, you'll feel better about giving them a little leeway.

That's how you understand organisations.

UNDERSTANDING SOCIETY

Amid all this talk of individual value and organisational behaviour, you might think the group doesn't matter. Actually, communities are *great*: while humans act as individuals, the human species is a social animal, and there's great value in taking part in society.

Here's how your social relationships relate to your life goals: they let you *trade value for value*. A father gives care and gets back joy. A businesswoman creates products and customers get benefit. A banker lends money and gets back interest.

The breaking point is when you start letting the group make decisions for you. Because that's where you mistake the individual *self* for the collective *identity*. And that way leads to non-actualisation. (How can you self-actualise with no self?)

To avoid this, understand all relationships are transactions between individuals. At all levels: kin, kith, and kountry, sorry, country. You invest in them; they pay you back. There's nothing cold or sinister about this; it's just how value works.

The other point in understanding society is **Dunbar's Number**.

Primate brains evolved to deal with three sizes of social group. 30-50 (the family or clan) 100-200 (the village) and up to 2500 (the broader tribe). What matters is the middle one.

Robin Dunbar found the human brain tops out at

about 150 close relationships. From the Paleo village to the business enterprise, a troop of 150 is the greatest bang per buck, the maximum number of individuals you can maintain stable, meaningful relationships with.

What's interesting is how well this number correlates with brain size. (Specifically, the neocortex, seat of language and reasoning—aka "thinking".) For gorillas, big bodied but small cortexed, it's 10. For chimps, a bit smarter, it's 40.

Proof positive: you are your brain, after all. So cultivate *your* village: work at maintaining 150 close relationships to feel most connected. Don't strive for more—but don't settle for less.

DISMISS THE STOOPIDS

In life you'll meet many stupid people. The correct approach: *be dismissive*.

Note stupid doesn't mean a lack of formal education. Some of the most schooled people are *extremely* stupid. And a lot of dropouts display great common sense and critical thinking. (Who, sight unseen, would you rather have in your apocalypse gang?)

Stupid is easy to recognise. One definition: someone who hurts himself a lot in a bid to hurt someone else a little. They're angry, vengeful, resentful, always playing the victim and preferring the lose-lose to the win-win. Because that's how they view the world: zero-sum, negative, and constantly out to get them.

Stupid people are guided by their S1, mistaking their vague feelings for absolute right or wrong. Stupid people do not use reason; therefore they cannot be reasoned *with*.

So the solution is simple. In real life, don't engage with them; ignore them. On social media, don't argue with them; block them. At work, if one is made your boss, leave that job.

As you move towards value, connect with as many good people as you can—but always dismiss the stupids. Completely and forever.

DISMISS EVERYBODY

There are a thousand demands on our time every day. Emails. Phone calls. Meetings. We're conditioned to treat any such interaction as worthy of a response.

They aren't, and you don't have to. Time is all any of us have; others have no right to steal it.

It's *okay* to turn down an invitation. It's *okay* to put the phone down with a brief "No thanks". It's *okay* to not engage, or decide, or take action, and leave it at that. You don't need to give reasons. It's *your* life, not theirs.

Save your time for the people who deserve it, by freeing yourself of those who don't. Be dismissive.

FAMILY AND CHILDREN

"How to do Life" is about *your* life. So it doesn't have much to say about family. Partners and children are not your property; they are individuals with rights, like you.

But it's a natural urge to have children. And luckily for the human species, many people do. So this section focusses on what you can do to make most difference to their lives: **education**.

As implied in "How to Learn", school tries to do too much. *Far* too much. Curriculums are cluttered with useless subjects like music, sport, and art.

(Yes. Useless. If they want to strum a guitar or kick a ball, great—but it's their hobby, not their homework.

And ignore any teacher who says otherwise.)

And when there's too little time for the basics—the three R's plus mathematics, history, physics, and literature—all the stuff you're layering on top fails to take.

"Financial literacy"? Try teaching them to add up. "Social and relationships?" Overthinking it. (Nobody ever had sex because a schoolteacher taught them how, except in a bad way.) And "citizenship classes"? My, how 1984.

Doing life doesn't need a university education. It's the years from birth to 18 that count. So don't start prepping your child for the Ivy League the day they burp into the world; campus universities might not even *exist* in 18 years' time. Go private if it works, homeschool if you have to, but focus 100% on teaching your child to *think*.

(A good start for the early years is Montessori; options nosedive from age 6. Leonard Peikoff's "Teaching Johnny to Think" is a useful guide.)

Yes, you'll probably be forced to use government schools. Some nations, incredibly, outlaw any other kind. (A basic rights violation, but governments do that.) Just don't make school the be-all and end-all of your child's education. Foster three skills, four subject areas, and logic, and the rest will happen naturally.

This means most of your kids' education has to happen outside school. So let them play, explore, take risks. Prefer self-guided discovery and problem-solving. Give them attention, but encourage responsibility. Don't provide solutions; provide learning opportunities. Teach a man to fish, and all that.

Above all, never forget that ultimately government schools follow a government agenda: to turn kids into "good citizens". And *their* idea of a "good citizen"—brutally, someone who puts the State's interests above their own—should not be yours.

Your life is *yours*. Make sure your children grow up to understand *their* lives are *theirs*.

ON ESTEEM

The fourth layer of Maslow's Pyramid is about confidence, feeling appreciated, social status, respect from others.

The esteem layer is the one that flirts with bullshit.

If you're doing life right, you'll be appreciated anyway: doing good work, for people you like, acting in accordance with your values. But a self-actualised person doesn't *need* the affirmation of others, because ultimately you're not doing it for them.

If you've learned how to think, fostered your 150 stable relationships, and built a body that roars, that's an end in itself. You don't need the approval of others.

FUCK GOVERNMENT.

Some time back, a gang of raiders had an idea. Instead of roving the countryside robbing villages, they'd simply rob the *same* village, again and again.

In time, the villagers noticed these raiders were chasing away *other* raiders, to protect their investment. So the villagers started reserving silver and grain to keep "their" raiders happy. And the raiders let the villagers keep some seed corn, so there'd be more to loot next harvest.

Today, we call this arrangement "government".

Beyond your family, village, and tribe—the Dunbar numbers—there's a larger network called "society", which government purports to make safe for you. But never believe for a second today's elected governments are any different to those raiders. Politicians are motivated by a single idea: wielding power over you.

And a man with power over you is a man who can stop you pursuing what you value.

This doesn't mean anarchy's a better choice. There *is* a role for government: ==protecting your individual rights==. A good government is limited in scope to this singular purpose.

There are no good governments.

But we can minimise their effects by, effectively, **telling them to fuck off**.

Don't work for the public sector. Don't work in a highly-regulated industry. Don't choose a career that's subject to constant inspections by clipboard-wielding bureaucrats. As far as you can, avoid dealing with the grey men of government *at all*.

Work for (or own) a private business. Live in private housing, pay for private health insurance, take out a private pension plan. Avoid contact with the law; maintain your privacy within it. Develop saleable skills that let you live without government help. And decide which red lines—corruption, dictatorship, economic policies—would make you *leave*. (The right skills will survive a move across borders.) If they arise, quietly pack up and go.

The best way to do life is to ==have as little to do with government as possible==.

FIND MEANINGFUL WORK

The apex of Maslow is **self-actualisation**—using your capabilities to turn *potential* into *reality*. (It doesn't happen by accident.) You get there by finding meaningful **work**.

Work—creating value for trade—is about more than putting food on the table. It's how you plan, grow, *live*. In meaningful work is the meaning of life.

You can work for yourself. You can work for someone else. But whatever you do, make sure it **aligns with your goals**. If it doesn't, it won't matter enough to you.

If you work for yourself, two books can help: a very short one in this series ("How to do Freelancing") and a very long one it introduces ("100 Days, 100 Grand").

At the core of both is a simple diagram called the ==Purposegram==, credited to Bencale and Shapland.

The Purposegram defines the ultimate value that brings meaning to your life and work—your **purpose**—as the intersection of four **Big Questions**.

What do you love? What do you do best? What does the market need? What will customers pay for?

Once you've worked out what connects these four questions, you'll be able to define what gives you your biggest buzz, your **flow**. It's "that thing you do", the activity that combines a sense of wonder and thrill with pride in your abilities and personal growth.

Yes, you *do* have one. Find it.

YOUR PURPOSE

When you've *found* your purpose—by developing your mind and body to the max, accepting reality and reason as absolutes, and pursuing what you value with meaningful work—**congratulations!** Because you've reached the successful state of living: **happiness**.

Happiness is the outcome of the actions in this little book. Note it doesn't tell you *what* you should value. Or *which* job you should take. Or *how* you should live. Because everybody's goals are different.

==It doesn't matter what your purpose *is*—just *have* one==.

And that's how to do life.

ABOUT CHRIS

Chris Worth is a London-based copywriter and author of the guide to effective freelancing **100 Days, 100 Grand**. Google it or head for 100days100grand.com.

At work, he creates campaigns and content backed by meaningful insights, mostly for technology clients. (He does the research and analysis too, btw—his USP.) Interests include adventure travel and extreme sports. He's lived in six countries, visited 60, and is a qualified sky *and* scuba diver with a passion for calisthenics and kettlebells. But he's never But he's never without his Kindle. See him at chrisdoescontent.com.

www.ingramcontent.com/pod-product-compliance
Lightning Source LLC
Chambersburg PA
CBHW081110080526
44587CB00021B/3529